LET'S VISIT ENGLAND

Let's visit ENGLAND

GARRY LYLE

BURKE

First published October 1973
New revised edition 1983
© Garry Lyle 1973

ACKNOWLEDGEMENTS

The author and publishers are grateful to the following individuals and organisations for permission to reproduce copyright illustrations:

British Aircraft Corporation; British Steel Corporation; British Tourist Authority; J. Allan Cash; Coventry City Council; Mike Dixon; Ford Motor Co. Ltd.; Greater London Council; Noeline Kelly; Keystone Press Agency Ltd.; London Transport Executive; National Farmers Union; Royal Shakespeare Theatre; J. Sainsbury Ltd.; Geoffrey Sherlock; John Topham Ltd.; Josiah Wedgwood & Sons Ltd.

The cover illustration of the Corps of Drums leaving Buckingham Palace is reproduced by permission of Camera Press Ltd.

CIP data

Lyle, Garry
   Let's visit England. – 2nd ed.
   1.   England – Social life and customs – Juvenile literature
   I.   Title
   942.082   DA566.4

ISBN 0 222 00919 5

Burke Publishing Company Limited
Pegasus House, 116–120 Golden Lane, London EC1Y 0TL, England.
Burke Publishing (Canada) Limited
Toronto, Onaterio, Canada.
Burke Publishing Company Inc.
540 Barnum Avenue, Bridgeport, Connecticut 06608, USA.
Filmset in 'Monophoto' Baskerville by Green Gates Studios, Hull, England.
Printed in Singapore by Tien Wah Press (Pte) Ltd.

Contents

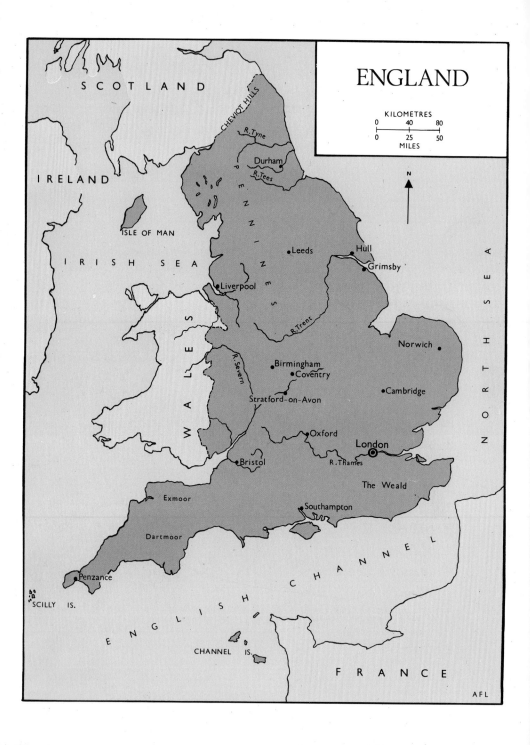

ENGLAND

KILOMETRES

0   40   80

0   25   50

MILES

SCOTLAND

CHEVIOT HILLS

R.Tyne

IRELAND

Durham

R.Tees

P E N N I N E S

ISLE OF MAN

Leeds

Hull

Grimsby

I R I S H   S E A

Liverpool

R.Trent

N O R T H   S E A

W A L E S

R.Severn

Norwich

Birmingham

Coventry

Cambridge

Stratford-on-Avon

Oxford

London

Bristol

R.Thames

The Weald

Exmoor

Southampton

Dartmoor

E N G L I S H   C H A N N E L

Penzance

SCILLY IS.

CHANNEL IS.

F R A N C E

N

AFL

What England Is

Not long ago, a travel agent in an English-speaking country advertised holiday tours to England. Very full tours they seemed, too. In fact, they seemed a little too full. The advertisement began:

Visit England this summer. See the Tower of London —
explore the Shakespeare Country—enjoy the Edinburgh Festival—
try a Devonshire tea—climb Mount Snowdon. . . .

Do you see why the advertisement seemed a little too full? Edinburgh is in Scotland. Mount Snowdon is in Wales. And the travel agent had forgotten that neither Scotland nor Wales is part of England.

However, it is not very likely that anyone took much notice of the mistake. People of other countries—and even some English people—often talk of England when they really mean Britain. And nobody is much confused by it. Still, people from the rest of Britain are sometimes a little offended. In any case, a visitor always travels more comfortably if he knows exactly where he is going. So, before *we* visit England, we had better be clear that England is a part—and only a part—of Great Britain, the largest of the British Isles.

That is only one way of saying what England is. If we want to place it in the wider world, we can call it a country of northern Europe. The British Isles lie off the northern shores of the European mainland, barely twenty-one miles (thirty-four kilometres) off at the nearest point. And if we want to say how it is related to its neighbours within the British Isles, we can call it a member country of the United Kingdom. England shares with Scotland, Wales and Northern Ireland a single democratic parliamentary government, under a royal head of state—at present, Queen Elizabeth II.

With Scotland and Wales, England also shares the whole 88,000 square miles (230,000 square kilometres) of Great Britain and a large number of small islands in the surrounding seas. But the shares are far from equal. England has about three-fifths of the total area. And these three-fifths are in the south, where the land is mainly more fertile and less ruggedly mountainous than it is in Wales and Scotland. On the whole, England has the best climate of the three countries, too— although English people might prefer to call it the least bad. They like to complain about their climate, and it certainly gives them something to complain about. There is rarely a week of the year without some rain, and the winters can be long, grey, foggy and sometimes severely cold. However, there is no doubt that most parts of Scotland and Wales are wetter, and most parts of Scotland colder. And when English weather does decide to be good it can be very good indeed, both in summer and in winter.

Besides having the best of Britain's weather, the best of its farmland and the easiest terrain for people moving about, England has the nearest seaports to the mainland of Europe.

A view of Chilham in Kent—a typical English village. This winter scene shows how cold and snowy the winter can be, even in the south of England

Along most of the 350 miles (560 kilometres) of its southern coastline, people are nearer to France than they are to London, their capital city. That has made travel and trade between England and the Continent very easy.

Because of all those advantages, England has always been the most prosperous and the most closely settled part of Great Britain. Great Britain's present population is over fifty-four million. Of that, England has about forty-six million—including many Scots and Welsh people who have found it easier to make a living in England than in their own countries.

Some of the Scots and Welsh belong to families who have lived in England for many generations, and think of themselves as English. For example, the surnames Jones, Evans and

9

Price are now among the commonest in England, but all three began in Wales. A very large number of other English people have surnames that were brought to England by settlers from other nations—Irish, French, Jews, Dutch and Italians, to name only a few. Think of the English playwright Terence Rattigan, the English engineer Isambard Brunel, the English statesman Benjamin Disraeli, the English poet John Betjeman and Ronnie Massarella, the English horseman and manager of Olympic show-jumping teams. None of those surnames came from the English language, but they are now quite at home in England.

The original homes of such names were neighbouring or not-too-distant countries, and the people who brought them

A London bus inspector — his family forms part of a multi-racial community

sank easily into the English background. But England's forty-six million people also include many who have come from more distant countries in recent years, and are rather more noticeable to visitors. If you travel by bus in London or one of the other big cities, you will probably buy your ticket from a Jamaican, or somebody born in one of the other islands of the West Indies. Your mail may be delivered by a Pakistani wearing a turban with his grey postman's uniform. And the cashier in the shop where you buy picture-postcards and souvenirs may be an Indian girl dressed in a bright sari. But perhaps the best way to see how many other countries are represented among the people of England is to stroll through the noisy streets of Soho, London's famous restaurant district. There, you would have no trouble in finding restaurants to serve you the national dishes of a different country for every meal of the day on every day of the week, or shops to sell you the ingredients for making the same dishes at home. And among the people who provide the food and who eat it you would also find natives of as many different countries, now living permanently in England.

Why have so many strangers come to England as settlers? One reason is that a large number hardly thought that they were strangers. Once—not so very long ago—England was the centre of the widespread British Empire, now the much smaller group of independent nations called the Common-wealth. In the years of the Empire, the peoples of all Empire countries were British subjects. As British subjects, they were

11

allowed to enter the United Kingdom whenever they wished, and to stay as long as they wished. So they could think of England as a second home, and that led many of them to make it their first home.

Another reason is that throughout their history the people of England have usually been ready to make room for strangers who could not live happily or safely in their own countries, or who had useful skills and ideas to offer. As early as the year 1156, groups of weavers from Flanders (now part of Belgium) had found homes in eastern England and were

Travellers on the London Underground—a typical mixture of people of different national and racial origin

building up an important cloth-making industry. As late as 1956, England offered a safe refuge to groups of Hungarians escaping from political persecution—and among their contributions to their new country were the heavyweight boxing champion Joe Bugner, and some economists who became advisers to the Government. Of course, the new arrivals rarely—and never wholly—continued to live as separate groups. In time, most of them mingled with the rest of the people, and many found English wives or husbands. So the modern English are a very mixed race. Every one of them must have at least one non-English ancestor. And because they are such a mixed race, they are also very mixed in physical appearance.

Still, if a visitor looks closely he will notice that most English people tend to be fair-skinned rather than dark, blue-eyed rather than brown-eyed, lean rather than plump, and a little taller than their Welsh neighbours or the peoples of southern Europe. That sounds much like a description of the earliest English, who themselves were new arrivals about fifteen hundred years ago.

Fifteen hundred years ago, the name England had not been invented. Great Britain, then known to civilized Europe as Britannia, had for over four hundred years been the furthest outpost of the Roman Empire. Most of the south had become settled, civilized and Christian. Roman colonists and Britons lived peacefully together, protected from unfriendly outsiders by Roman soldiers. But Rome—like Britain in this century,

It is easy to study
the variety of a
London crowd in
one of the city's
many busy street
markets. This
is the famous
market in the
East End known
as Petticoat Lane

though for different reasons—gradually gave up her empire. Over the years after A.D. 410, the colonies of southern Britannia were left to govern themselves, and to defend themselves. From then on, the outsiders began to come inside.

Among the outsiders were some groups of pagan, semi-civilized sea-raiders called Angli, who came from a poor and overcrowded stretch of coastland in what is now Germany. Finding the east coast of Britain much more attractive, the Angli—or Angles—stopped raiding and began to settle. And their settlements came to be known as Angle-land, later shortened to England. Meanwhile, other raiders from the

14

German coastlands had been landing and settling in the south. These were Jutes (who stayed in the south-east corner that is now the county of Kent) and Saxons who moved slowly northward until they met Angles spreading slowly in from the east. They had to move slowly, because the Roman Britons did not give up their land without a struggle. At least once, at a place called Mount Badon, the invaders were severely beaten, and prevented from going further for a long time. But the invaders had come to stay. At last, most of the Roman Britons were driven northward into Scotland or westward into Wales and what are now the English counties of Devon and Cornwall.

This church was built by the Saxons, although the windows were put in at a later date

The rest were lost among the newcomers. South Britannia had become the land of the Angles, Saxons and Jutes; and because the Angles were the most powerful and widely spread of the newcomers, people began to call the whole country England.

As the generations went by, both the Britons and the new settlers forgot exactly where the battlefield called Mount Badon was. But they remembered that the Roman-British fighting-men had been led by a very popular Briton named Artorius, who had perhaps been trained as an officer in the Roman cavalry. Many stories—most of them made up—were told about him. Those stories grew into the famous legends of King Arthur and his Knights of the Round Table, which sometimes turn the facts completely upside down and make Arthur a leader of the Saxons.

Though the Angles, Saxons and Jutes were related peoples, and spoke different dialects of the same language, they did not at first live as one nation, or even as friendly neighbours. More often than not, each was at war with the other, until finally the Saxons of the south-west became so powerful that their kings were ruling all England. By then, Angles, Saxons and Jutes were all calling themselves English. They had also become Christian. Although Christianity had not made them more peaceful, it had made them more civilized—so civilized that they themselves began to attract sea-raiders.

Like the Angles, Saxons and Jutes, these new raiders came across the North Sea from the mainland of Europe. Their homes were on the cold and uncomfortable shores of what are

16

now known as the Scandinavian countries. Tall, big-boned, blue-eyed people, mainly with red or very fair hair, they called themselves Vikings. But the English knew them as Danes.

During most of two unhappy centuries the Danes terrorized, settled—and for twenty-six years even ruled—England. Their settlements were on the east coast; many places there—for instance, the fishing-port of Grimsby—still keep their Danish names. The English language still has many of their words, too—everyday words like *egg* and *happy* and *she*. And, of course, some of them married among the English, just as some of the Angles, Saxons and Jutes had married among the remaining Roman Britons. So the English had already become a mixture of several peoples. Another people—itself a mixture —was soon to be added. In 1066, perhaps the best-known date in English history, England was invaded, conquered and taken over by Normans from northern France.

The Normans were a much more advanced people than the earlier invaders from northern Europe. It was they who really put England on the road to becoming what it is. By strong government and strong defences, they gave it the chance to grow without fear of attacks from outside or wars inside. By introducing new ideas, new ways of working and new trades, they made the country more productive, and more widely productive. Because of their links with France, they "brought England into Europe", and so began its change from a backward and still rather primitive country to one of the world's great powers—for a time the world's greatest power.

How England Grew

People sometimes wonder why the English language often has one word for the meat of an animal and another word for the animal itself: why, between the farm and the meal-table, sheep should become mutton, calf should become veal, and pig should become pork. It does seem rather an odd change—but perhaps not quite so odd to those who notice that the words *mutton*, *veal* and *pork* look very like some French words for sheep, calf and pig, and then remember England's Norman invaders.

The Norman invaders spoke an early form of French, and their descendants were a very long time changing fully to English—so long that when the change did come the English language itself had changed. Like the speakers, the English and French languages had mixed, and many of the old English

The Tower of London, as it looks today. The original building was Norman but it has since been added to at various times

words had been replaced by French words. For instance, before 1066 the group of people chosen to advise the king and make laws for the country had the old English name *moot*. But by 1266 it had—as it still has—the French name *parliament*.

However, the changing of old English words for French words answers only half the question about pairs of words like *sheep* and *mutton*. Sheep meat certainly came to be called mutton because the word *mutton* (spelt rather differently) is a French word for sheep. But the animals themselves were never called muttons in English. The reason for that is the relationship between the English and the Normans in the first years of Norman rule. Then, it was the English who farmed the animals, but the Normans who ate the meat. So the mixed language kept the English word for the English end of the process, and took the French word for the Norman end. And in that there is a very fair picture of everyday life in early Norman England. The English still worked the land, but the Normans now owned it, and took the best of its products.

The English could do little to resist their Norman masters. The Normans were too powerful. Perhaps, too, the English were not very willing to try. They had a very hard life, but it was also a secure and peaceful one. And in England peaceful security had been rare for a long time. Still, the Normans did not have it all their own way. A few of the English resisted them, usually living as outlaws in the forests and the wilder parts of the country. With their resistance began the many stories of English outlaw heroes like Hereward the Wake and

Robin Hood. But the resisters are much more successful in the stories than they were in real life. They achieved very little against the Normans; and when life grew better for the English it grew better because the Normans and the other Frenchmen who followed them gradually began to think of themselves as English, too.

They had good reason to think so. England was now their home. More and more of them had married among the English, and had seen their children marry among the English. To their children's children the Normans of France seemed foreigners. Because of that, some of the old English ideas and customs began to return, including the very important idea that the king should obey the law, respect the rights and freedom of his subjects, and allow at least some of his subjects a share in governing the country. Since 1066, the kings of England had rarely been inclined to do those things. When the new English began to demand them they led, in the year 1215, to the signing of Magna Carta, the Great Charter.

In the Great Charter, King John promised to obey the law, to govern by the law, and to allow his subjects their ancient rights and freedoms. He did not mean to keep the promise; and he soon broke it. So did some later kings. But they were not allowed to do so for long. The signing of the Charter had shown that the king's subjects could control the king, and their control grew steadily stronger.

The people who forced King John to sign the Charter were the barons, the great land-holders. They were thinking mainly

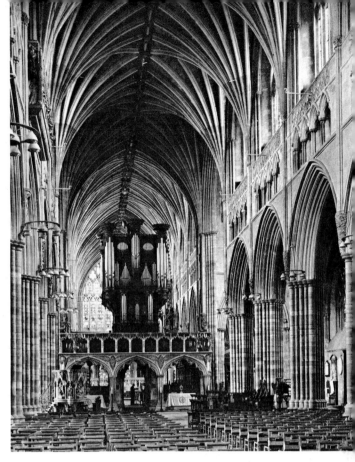

Exeter Cathedral
—an example of
some of England's
most beautiful
architecture.
As the political
life of the country
developed, so too
did the religious
and cultural life

of their own rights, and did not much care how the rest of the people fared. But, in order to control the king, they needed support from the rest of the people. So the people were represented when the Charter was signed, and were promised that in future they would be represented at national councils called to advise the king. At first, that promise was not always kept. But from it—over a very long time and after much struggle—grew the parliamentary system by which England, and the whole United Kingdom, are now governed.

21

Under the English parliamentary system, the power is in the hands of all the people. Their representatives are the members of the House of Commons, chosen every five years at elections in which every citizen who has passed his or her eighteenth birthday may vote. There is also a House of Lords —a survival from the barons' councils of Magna Carta times— which is not chosen by the people. But the House of Lords has no power to make laws by itself, or to prevent what the House of Commons wishes to do. Only the monarch, the reigning king or queen, has power to stand in the way of the House of Commons, and that power is never used. The monarch is expected always to take the advice of ministers who themselves come from the House of Commons, or who support the policy of the ruling party in the House of Commons.

Whether they are monarchies or republics, most countries

In modern England there is no conflict between monarch and subjects. Here Queen Elizabeth II is shown in procession on her way to open a new session of Parliament

of western Europe and many others now have parliamentary systems similar to the one which grew up in England over the centuries after King John signed the Great Charter. In those countries, representative government often came very suddenly, sometimes after revolution or civil war. Only in England did the idea grow up with the country. So the old-established parliament of England became the model for newly-established parliaments in every continent. In the eyes of people who like to be governed by their own freely-elected representatives, that is the greatest of England's many contributions to the modern world.

While the new Norman-English people were struggling to control their kings, the kings were usually more concerned with controlling their neighbours. They invaded Wales, where descendants of the Roman Britons were living under the rule of their own princes and, after many years of fighting, the Welsh princes were replaced by the son of an English king. That is why the eldest son of the English monarch is still called the Prince of Wales. From Wales, the Norman-English kings invaded Ireland, a kingdom which the Romans had never entered, and there—with the help of some Irish—they made themselves masters. They also invaded Scotland, but from Scotland—like the Romans before them—they were driven back.

England never did conquer Scotland. Scotland remained a separate and independent kingdom until 1603, when Queen Elizabeth I of England died. Queen Elizabeth I had no children, and no closer relation than her distant cousin King James VI of Scotland. So King James VI of Scotland became King James I of England, and that made the whole island of Great Britain—England, Scotland and Wales—the united kingdom that it still is.

King James also became king of Ireland, which was still under English rule, and which remained so until 1922. Then, most of the country became an independent state, and later a republic (Eire), leaving six counties in the north as a separate country within the United Kingdom.

With that, it is time to remember again what the travel agent forgot—a visit to England is not a visit to the whole of the British Isles. It is impossible to visit England without hearing something of Scotland, Wales and Ireland. So much of England's story is their story, too. But England is still a separate country. It looks different naturally, and it has grown in a different way. The people themselves are notice-ably different. Many of their customs, their likes and dislikes, their ways of thinking and living are different. As we have seen, even the climate changes a little when we cross the Cheviot Hills into Scotland, or the Bristol Channel into Wales. So from now on we will forget the rest of the British Isles, and keep within the traditional counties of England.

The word *county* came into the English language in the same way as the word *mutton*, from the language of the Norman-French. It replaced the old English word *shire*, which still remains in the names of some counties—Yorkshire and

Lancashire, for instance. It also remains hidden in the word *sheriff*, which is a shortened form of *shire-reeve*. The original sheriffs were officers who represented the king in the English shires. And the original shires were divisions of the kingdom made to ease the work of local government.

Local government is still the only practical reason for England's county divisions. County councils, elected by all residents aged eighteen years and over, do much of the work which in some other countries is done by the central government. But modern England has developed in ways that could hardly have been imagined when the present county boundaries were fixed. Areas which once had large populations are emptying. Areas which had small populations can now count their people in millions. New towns have grown up so quickly that their names cannot always be found on fairly recent maps. Old towns and villages have spread out to join each other and make great, sprawling cities. Industrial estates and motorways and airports have been cutting into farmland and wasteland.

Many of those developments could not be managed efficiently by a system of local government which grew in a very different England. So, since 1974, there have been some changes in the old county divisions, and in the smaller local government divisions within each county. But the changes have made very little difference to the way in which the people of England live, work, learn and amuse themselves. And that is what we are now going to see.

England at Work—Factories

England not only led the world in the development of parliamentary government. It also led the world into the changes that are now called the Industrial Revolution. The changes began a little more than two hundred years ago, when England was still mainly a farming country, and for its most important manufacturing industry used a raw material from the farms—wool. The wool was spun into yarn by hand. The yarn was woven into cloth on looms that were worked by hand. Sometimes, the looms stood side by side in small factories, usually in towns or villages near the sheep farms. More often the weaver, like the spinner, worked in his own cottage. But wherever the yarn was spun and the cloth woven, it was hand work all the way.

There was nothing unusual about that. Before the Industrial Revolution, all machines were simple, and most were light enough to be powered by human muscles. The others—flour grinders, for instance—relied on wind or water. Machines which can take their power from wind or water do more work in less time than machines powered by human muscles. After about 1770 some newly invented machines allowed water-power to replace human muscles in the English cloth-making industry. Then, when the spinners and weavers were hardly used to water-power, people at last began to see a practical use for something that they had known since the first lid rattled on a pot of boiling water—the power of steam.

26

Dyeing wool in West Yorkshire

Nowadays, the credit for taking the first steps with steam-power is often given to James Watt, a Scotsman. But Thomas Newcomen and other Englishmen were a step ahead of him. Their steam-powered engines for pumping water from mines gave Watt the lead to inventing steam-powered engines that would drive machinery for any kind of work. It was Englishmen, too, who invented the spinning and weaving machines that could be driven by Watt's engines.

That was the beginning of the so-called Industrial Revolution, when many thousands of people left farms and village workshops and cottage industries (like hand-spinning and weaving) to become factory workers in smoky, congested

27

industrial towns. It was also the beginning of the England that visitors see today.

Some of the industrial towns started with the changes in industry. They grew up as long terraces of red-brick or grey-stone workers' cottages built back to back near a new factory—or mill, as spinning and weaving factories are usually called. Other towns—like Leeds and Bradford—were already well-established centres of the cloth-making industry. Leeds and Bradford are the biggest of a group of wool towns in western Yorkshire, below the central slopes of the bare but beautiful "backbone of England"—the Pennine Range.

The whole stretch of the Pennines has always been an important sheep-raising area, but the wool towns are con-centrated near the central slopes because the natural water there is soft. It is much easier to wash the grease from raw wool with soft water than with hard water. However, it is neither the Pennine wool nor the soft water that has made Leeds and Bradford by far the biggest woollen manufacturing towns in modern England. Coal and iron have done that. The steam that powered the Industrial Revolution used coal for fuel. The machines that they drove, and the engines themselves, were made of iron and its product steel. So the steam-powered industries kept costs down by concentrating in areas where coal and iron were mined—areas like the west of Yorkshire. That is also why the cathedral city of Norwich, in Norfolk on the east coast, now lives mainly by making shoes, electrical goods and mustard. Norwich was for many years the centre of the cloth-making industry begun by weavers from Flanders over eight hundred years ago. But it is far from a coalfield, and its looms could not compete with the steam-powered mills of Yorkshire. Nor could the looms of Devonshire and some other old weaving centres with good local wool but no local coal.

Over the Pennines from Yorkshire, in the southern half of Lancashire, the woollen industry died out for a different reason. In fact, it had nearly died out before the Industrial Revolution started. South Lancashire borders on the wide River Mersey, now famous for the pair of road tunnels beneath it, and for the type of pop music called *the Mersey beat*.

The Mersey beat started in Liverpool, the big seaport city near the mouth of the Mersey, at the Lancashire end of the road tunnels. But Liverpool was a famous exporting town long before it began to export pop music. During the eighteenth century, one of its main exports was people—emigrants sailing to the colonies of the British Empire that became the United States of America. On the voyage back to Liverpool, the ships were often loaded with raw cotton grown in the colonies. Some of the Lancashire spinners and weavers were already working with cotton imported from Egypt. So now, with so much more coming in from America, the whole cloth-making area turned from wool to cotton. A few of the cloth-makers also turned their thoughts to ways of using the raw cotton more quickly. It was they who invented most of the machinery that crossed the Pennines into Yorkshire and changed the woollen industry. And because south Lancashire also had coal and iron, the coming of steam-power kept the English cotton industry concentrated there.

Many of south Lancashire's cotton products were exported, from the spreading docks of Liverpool. Before they went to the docks the goods were sent from the weaving towns to warehouses in Manchester, a plain and businesslike city about thirty-five miles (fifty-six kilometres) inland, on a tributary of the Mersey. That took Manchester's name around the world. Shopkeepers in many countries came to call the cotton goods department "the Manchester department", because the goods nearly all had Manchester labels. After 1894, it was also very likely that the goods had come direct from Manchester. Seven years of very difficult engineering work had made Manchester a seaport, connected to the Mersey by a ship canal thirty-five miles (fifty-six kilometres) long, and deep enough for ocean-going vessels.

Manchester is also a manufacturing city. Many of its factories make the machinery, equipment and chemicals used in spinning and weaving. And those too are often exported by way of the Manchester Ship Canal. As a result, the south Lancashire cotton industry is not as big or as prosperous as it was. Other countries have bought Manchester machinery and used it to make some of their own "Manchester" goods. A little of what was lost to the cotton industry has been made up by weaving and exporting products of a new raw material— man-made fibres such as terylene. When man-made fibres were invented, coal was no longer important to the cloth industries. The machinery could be powered by oil fuels and electricity. So many of the factories using man-made fibres are well away from the coalfields. Some were established in places like the old market town of Tiverton in Devonshire, which once lost a prosperous woollen industry because the nearest coal was not near enough.

When oil fuels and electricity became an alternative to coal, many other factories were sited away from the coalfields, especially in the counties around the city of London, where more than one third of England's people now live—often with very serious housing and transport problems. But most of the country's manufacturing industries are still where the Industrial Revolution put them—near the coalfields and the iron mines of the northern and midland counties.

Many of the iron mines are worked out now. Today, most of England's iron comes from other countries. But the coal mines are still very important. Their coal helps to generate some of the electricity that has partly replaced steam-power. And it is much used in making chemicals—including the dyes that colour wool, cotton and man-made fibres for the cloth industries. That has put some very big chemical works among the cotton towns on the south Lancashire coalfield, and in Cheshire just across the Mersey. The works on the Cheshire side are there because of Cheshire's salt, which is as useful to the chemical industry as it is in the kitchen and at the table.

Salt has been mined in Cheshire for at least two thousand years. Yet the mines are still supplying nearly all the salt that

Britain uses, and much that is used in places as far away as eastern Asia. The deposits lie deep below the valley of the River Weaver. An odd thing about them is that the miners do not usually go down to the salt. They make the salt come up to them. By pumping water down to the salt they dissolve it, and then pump the salty water back to the surface. There, the water is evaporated until only the salt is left.

The River Weaver flows into the Mersey, and from it a narrow canal tunnels through a spur of the Pennine Range to join the River Trent, which flows through a big coalfield in the north of Staffordshire. Before English engineers like George Stephenson had thought of putting steam-engines on wheels to make railway engines, that canal was achieved by another Englishman with a well-known name—Josiah Wedgwood. If Josiah Wedgwood's name is not well-known to you, you may find it on the underside of a cup or a plate, or on a colour chart against a colour called Wedgwood blue. After more than two hundred years, Josiah Wedgwood's firm is still making chinaware near the River Trent, much of it in the Wedgwood blue colour. It was the needs of the Trent's chinaware industry that caused the Trent and Mersey Canal to be dug.

Chinaware and earthenware—usually called pottery—are made from special clays baked under carefully controlled heat in tall kilns shaped like milk bottles. There was clay on the north Staffordshire coalfield and, of course, plenty of coal to fire the kilns. That is why the pottery industry began there.

But the clay was not very good—certainly not good enough to make chinaware of high quality. The nearest clay of that kind was in the far south-west of England, where there is no coal. It was easier to bring the clay to the coal than the coal to the clay. Before the days of rail and motor transport, that meant a long sea journey round the coast to Liverpool. So Josiah Wedgwood had the Trent and Mersey Canal built so that the clay could travel on water all the way to the kilns. By the same canal, the finished pottery could travel to Liverpool for shipment abroad —a much less dangerous journey for fragile goods than the bumpy ride over the hills on waggon or packhorse. From that grew the district known to all English people as the Potteries— a stretch of nine miles (fourteen kilometres) along the River Trent where the skyline is mainly kilns, and most of the 250,000 people are connected in one way or another with producing the world's greatest output of crockery and other baked clay goods.

The Trent and Mersey Canal joins the River Trent twice, first at the Potteries and then, about fifty miles (eighty kilometres) down the river's curving valley, at the lacemaking town of Nottingham whose sheriff had so much trouble from Robin Hood in the stories. At Nottingham, a canal-boat loaded at Liverpool can carry on down the Trent into the River Humber, and unload at the port of Hull on the other side of England. On the way back, it could turn into other lengths of the country-wide canal system that carried nearly all the raw materials and products of England's growing industries

Wedgwood pottery in traditional designs

when there was neither road nor rail transport. Since then, much of the system has been closed, or kept open only for pleasure boats, but the rest still carries nearly five million tons (tonnes) of goods every year.

What crockery is to the workers of north Staffordshire, hardware is to the workers of south Staffordshire. Like the north, south Staffordshire has a rich coalfield. It also lies close to another one, over the county border in Warwickshire. And both are in easy reach of iron. With Birmingham in Warwickshire, south Staffordshire was a busy iron-working district long before the Industrial Revolution. James Watt came to Birmingham to build his steam-engines. With the Industrial Revolution the district became the world's biggest supplier of

34

metal goods—metal goods of all kinds and sizes, from buttons to buses. Over the years, local people visiting the countries of Asia have often bought very oriental-looking trays, brooches and daggers to take home as souvenirs, only to find that their souvenirs were made in Birmingham.

The Industrial Revolution also brought to the district a name that was well-deserved—the Black Country. Smoke from foundries and factories blackened the sky. Soot blackened buildings and open spaces—and even hands if they happened to touch a wall. One sooty town led quickly into another over an area of two hundred square miles (five hundred square kilometres). But the Black Country is now much less black than it used to be. Smokeless fuels and careful control of factories and foundries have done that, without reducing the vast

A lock on one of England's many canals

The old—the fourteenth-century Minstrel's Gallery of St. Mary's Guildhall in Coventry

amount of hardware that the factories and foundries turn out.

Oddly enough, a Warwickshire town which is just outside the Black Country but does "Black Country" work also makes silk ribbons. You may know its name—Coventry—because the story of Lady Godiva and her hard-hearted husband is said to have happened there about twenty years before the Normans invaded England. That makes Coventry a town with a long history, and—unlike some of England's other big industrial towns—it has some very old buildings. Several of them go back to the century after the Great Charter was signed. It also has a famous new building—a cathedral opened in 1962, to replace one destroyed when the town was bombed fiercely during the Second World War. The cathedral's very modern design brings many thousands of visitors to see it, but Coventry is perhaps better known for its big share of the million or more motor vehicles made in England every year, and for its work in aircraft construction.

Another, and bigger, aircraft construction centre is the West Country city of Bristol. Although it is one of England's main ports, Bristol is not on the sea. It is connected to the

And the new— Coventry Cathedral

estuary of the River Severn by the Severn's narrow but navigable tributary the River Avon. Through the Severn and the Bristol Channel, the Avon leads to the Atlantic Ocean and a more direct sea route to America than the route from Liverpool. So Bristol ships were sailing to America and trading with America long before the cotton trade made Liverpool into England's chief port for transatlantic shipping. In fact, a Bristol captain—born in Italy—may have reached the mainland of America before Christopher Columbus. Columbus reached the islands of the West Indies in 1492, but he did not go further until 1498, and in that year John Cabot of Bristol was also on the American mainland. Three hundred and forty years later, Bristol built the first steamship designed for regular Atlantic crossings; much of the cargo unloaded at its docks still comes from America and the West Indies. Among this cargo every year are many shiploads of raw materials for Bristol's big paper-making and tobacco industries, and several million bunches of bananas.

Luckily for Bristol, it is near one of the few considerable coalfields south of the Black Country, and so had no difficulty in keeping up with the Industrial Revolution. Indeed, visitors cannot help seeing one of the Industrial Revolution's great achievements on the city's own skyline—the beautiful Clifton suspension bridge, designed by Isambard Brunel, across the deep gorge of the Avon.

Until 1974 Bristol was not only a city but also a very small county—so small that some of its docks and shipyards and

The Clifton suspension bridge

many of its factories and engineering works were outside the city limits, in the counties of Gloucester and Somerset. However, those parts of Gloucester and Somerset have, since 1974, been added to Bristol to make a new county called Avon, after the river which runs through it.

If you look at a map of the English midlands, you will see a River Avon near Coventry. It flows south-westward through the town of Stratford-upon-Avon, Shakespeare's birthplace, to join the River Severn at Tewkesbury, a farming centre with some old buildings half-timbered in the style of the first Queen Elizabeth's reign. But that Avon is not the Bristol Avon.

39

Building the "Concord", in a factory just outside Bristol

Rather confusingly for visitors, Avon is the name of two tributaries of the Severn, and if you look more widely over a detailed map you will find that it is also the name of several other rivers. That is the result of a mistake by the early English settlers. In the ancient British language, and in the modern Welsh language, *avon* (or *afon*) is the word for river. But in some districts the English settlers took it to be only the name of the local river. So when we talk about the River Avon we are really saying "the River River".

The Avon that flows near Coventry and through Warwickshire rises in a neighbouring county, Northamptonshire. Not far from its source are several more towns whose metal industries link them with the Black Country. Among them is

Corby (a Danish name) which, in spite of a long history, is a "new town". With about twenty-six other "new towns", it has been developed by the United Kingdom government to stop some of the older industrial areas from becoming over-crowded, and to give industrial workers more pleasant surroundings and more comfortable living conditions.

Corby takes the iron for its industries from a long ridge of ironstone hills whose mines also help to supply the true Black Country. Beyond Northamptonshire, the hills carry on towards the north and, before we come to their end, we are back in Yorkshire, at another manufacturing centre on another coalfield. The centre, set against a fine part of the Pennines called the Peak District, is Sheffield, whose name you will almost certainly have seen on knife blades. Though

Pouring molten iron into a steel converter in Corby

Sheffield makes metal goods of many kinds—as well as sweets and snuff—blade-making is its speciality. Scissors and swords, penknives and ploughshares, anything of any size that needs a sharp steel cutting edge can be safely ordered from Sheffield. But for a ship or a railway track or an oil-rig—any really heavy steel goods—you must go further north still. Those things are products of the towns on the Northumberland and Durham coalfield—the towns along the Rivers Tees, Wear and Tyne which flow into the North Sea—or of Barrow back across the Pennines in Lancashire.

If you go to Darlington on the Tees, you can see a very early product of England's heavy industries—railway engine Number 1, built by the railway pioneer George Stephenson. Number 1 was the first engine on the first passenger railway in the world. Opened in 1825, the line ran between Darlington and Stockton, eleven miles (eighteen kilometres) further down the Tees.

Within twenty-five years, all the main towns of England were connected by railway. And because railways could carry coal and raw materials cheaply and quickly, manufacturing industries spread with them—often to railway junctions where the railway companies had set up workshops to build and repair their engines and rolling stock. The industrial towns of Crewe in Cheshire and Swindon in Wiltshire, and the Clapham Junction area on the south side of London, all grew from very small beginnings in that way.

When the first railways were laid, Swindon was a farming

42

Shipyards on the River Tyne

village, Clapham was a residential village, and Crewe was a single house.

In modern England, railways are losing some of their importance to motorways, and fast motor transport is opening still more parts of the country to industrial development. But are there any more parts? Knowing that England is among Europe's smaller countries, people further away sometimes imagine it as one unbroken industrial area already; a flying visit to Manchester or Birmingham or London does little to change their minds. But this is a longer visit, so we have time to see how wrong they are.

43

England at Work—Farms and Fisheries

For every ten English people who work in manufacturing industries, there is only one farm-worker. But that one is very important, although his work cannot clothe and feed the other ten completely. Much more than half of England's food must now come from other countries. So too must about four-fifths of its wool for spinning and weaving, and most of the leather for its shoe-making industry. And the cost of all those foods and raw materials must be set against payments coming in for the vast quantity of manufactured goods that England sends abroad. This gives the relatively few English farm-workers a major share in making their country prosperous. English factories cannot avoid importing many of their raw materials. England has run out of some and has never had others. But English farms can provide food; and the more they provide, the less England has to rely on—and pay for—the farm produce of other countries.

It was not the loss of farmland to factories and factory towns that made the English rely on other countries for most of their food. Much to the surprise of those who cross the country expecting to find an unbroken industrial area, the industrial areas take up very little of it. Sheep still graze over the whole length of the Pennines—the mountain range which runs from

Sheep in pens at a market-day sale

north to south, like a backbone. Along the three hundred miles (480 kilometres) of railway between London in the south-east and Penzance in the far south-west, the average distance between the bigger towns is well over thirty miles (forty-eight kilometres), and the rest is mainly farmland. The Weald district—about three thousand square miles (7,600 square kilometres) of four south-eastern counties—is still rightly called "the garden of England". Through much of Norfolk and Suffolk, an area bigger than the Weald, there is little to be seen but wheat, barley and sugar-beet fields. The west midland county of Hereford has long stretches of apple orchards and cattle pastures. Even in the Black Country there are farms between the foundries, and once you are south of Birmingham you can travel to many places on the English Channel coast

Harvesting in Norfolk

knowing that any town you pass through will be a market town for farmers.

To put all that as one simple fraction, very nearly four-fifths of England is still farmland, and still used as farmland. Also, most of the four-fifths is very fertile, and very productive if the weather allows it to be so. When the first Romans came to what is now England over two thousand years ago, their leader Julius Caesar reported that crops were quick to grow but slow to ripen. Modern English farmers know exactly what he meant. In the growing season—late spring and early summer—they can usually rely on having the regular rain and the warm air that bring crops on very quickly. But in the ripening season of late summer there is often too little dry

46

weather and warm sun to make a good harvest. Sometimes well-ripened crops are ruined by heavy rains that come suddenly, right on harvest time.

However, for most English farmers in most years the harvests are good, and they are growing bigger with the use of modern machinery and modern farming methods. They could certainly provide all the main foods for the population of England as it was in the early years of the Industrial Revolution. But since then there has been what some people nowadays call a "population explosion". In the early years of the Industrial Revolution, England had about eight million people. Now, there are more than twice as many in London and the south-eastern counties alone, and nearly six times as many in the whole country. That is the real reason why the farms of England cannot provide the people of England with three good meals a day.

Picking hops which will be used to brew English beer

English farmers have been doing their best. They once used much fertile land in the south of England for grazing sheep. But sheep do not need fertile land. They graze well on soil too thin to be cultivated. So to find a sheep flock in the south of England nowadays you must climb the dry slopes of the low limestone hills that give the south-east its backbone. The old sheep pastures grow grain, fruit, vegetables and the hop plant that is used in making the Englishman's favourite drink—beer. Good crops—especially potatoes for England's famous "chips with everything"—are also grown on farmland that has been made available by draining wide areas of marsh on the east coast. Some farmers have even given themselves more soil for food crops by digging out the thick hedges which for centuries have been grown as fences between fields.

New crops have appeared, too. Sugar-beet was hardly known in England before 1920. Now about one third of the country's sugar comes from its beet farms. That one third, by the way, would make a very large hill if it were all piled together. English people generally like sweet tea and coffee, sweet puddings and sweet breakfast foods, and it is said that they eat more toffees and chocolates than any other nation.

Of course, English farm produce has also been greatly increased by factory-made plant and animal foods, and by modern farming methods. Many of these methods were first tried out on English farms, and every English market town has its agricultural machinery dealers and repair shops, although some English farmers are not as enthusiastic about engine-

48

power as they were. They claim that for some farm jobs the old-fashioned horse has proved to be just as efficient, and less expensive to run.

By the standards of some other countries, English farms are not very big. The average is about eighty acres (thirty-two hectares), and many are as small as twenty acres (eight hectares) or even less. Most farmers concentrate their work on one particular crop or animal—for instance, grain or soft fruits in the east where the late summer is likely to be dry; dairy cattle or apples and pears in the west where summer rain keeps the pastures green, and the apples and pears from falling before they are ripe. But the grain farmer and the fruit farmer often keep a cow or two and some pigs, while dairy farmers sow a small area with turnips and haymaking grasses to feed their cows in winter, and they often grow a grain or a fruit crop for marketing, too.

In the north, the farms and the fields within them are often divided by finely made dry stone walls—that is, walls in which rough stones are held together by their own shapes and weight, without the help of mortar. In the south, the traditional hedge, often of holly or hazel, is the main divider, but good hedging is a skilled craft, and farm workers have grown less willing to learn it. When hedges need repair or replacement, many farmers are now choosing fence wire. In addition to hedges (or instead of hedges), fields in the wetter districts are often divided by ditches which also drain the land. In these, as unwary visitors may find to their discomfort, a watery bottom

49

may be hidden under a growth of wild plants that is much less solid than it looks.

Nowadays, some English farmers like to live in town houses, perhaps in a city suburb, and drive to and from their work. But the majority still prefer a full-time country life, and they live on their farms. The farmhouse often makes one side of a rough square, with barns, garage, cowshed, dairy, pig and poultry houses filling the other sides. The space inside the square—the farmyard—is large and often mainly unpaved. In the rainy English climate a visitor learns very quickly why the most noticeable part of an English farmer's clothing is a pair of knee-high rubber boots.

Most farmhouses are two-storied and roomy, with large and comfortable kitchens where the farmer and his family usually eat breakfast and perhaps most of their other meals. The breakfasts are large, too. On all dairy farms and many others, the farmer has already been at work for two hours before the meal. As the children may have a long bus ride before they begin their day at school, they like to leave the farm feeling as well fed as their father.

If a farmer has enough land for him to employ farm workers, the workers sometimes live on the farm, and have their meals in the farmhouse. More often, and especially if the farmworker is married, his home is a cottage in a village near by. There are very few English farms which are more than a short distance from a village, or a hamlet as a very small village is called.

50

Most village people make their living from the farms round about them. If they do not work on farms, they are shop-keepers serving farms, or craftsmen ready to do the many occasional jobs that farmers cannot manage themselves—jobs like carpentry, machine repair, harvesting, hedging, ditching and thatching. Thatch is the traditional material for farm and village roofs in many parts of England, but a visitor is now very lucky if he sees a thatched roof on anything but a cottage shown on a picture postcard. Like hedging, thatching is a skilled craft, and many people who might have become thatchers have taken their skill to town work. Besides, a slate roof or a tiled roof is less expensive, and needs repair less often.

Not all of England's villages are farming villages. On most of the many small harbours along the coastline there is at least

A blacksmith at work

one fishing village. Many of them are also summer holiday places, but their all-the-year-round work is fishing. Usually, the boats of a village fishing fleet are small in size and in number. They work in local waters, rarely far from home. But there are also some very large fleets of bigger vessels—trawlers and drifters which go away for weeks at a time, fishing widely over the North Sea and far out into the Atlantic. Those fleets work from seaport towns like Grimsby, the old east coast Danish settlement which now calls itself the biggest fishing port in the world. Their yearly catch, with the catch of the village fleets, adds over four hundred thousand tons (more than 406,000 tonnes) of fish to England's food supply.

Like most farm workers and other wage-earners, most crewmen of the fishing fleets belong to trade unions, which have done a great deal to improve their conditions of work and increase their wages. Trade unions as they are known now are a result of the Industrial Revolution and, like the Industrial Revolution itself, they began in England. It was only when factory work brought people together in large groups that they could combine to force a fair return for their work, and fair conditions of work. Their success helped farm labourers, fishing crews and other scattered workers to better their own pay and conditions. That, in its turn, has done much towards making the home conditions that a visitor will find in England.

England at Home

To some visitors, it seems strange that so many English people live in houses. They know that England could use more farmland. Yet they find that even the seventeen million people crowded into the south-east are mainly house-dwellers. So they cannot help feeling that all those houses are rather wasteful. Would it not have been better to build what the Americans call "high-rise" apartments—tall blocks of flats which each hold as many families as a whole street of houses—and leave the rest of the land to farmers?

The visitors are not alone in thinking like that. Some English people have the same idea. In the 1950s "high-rise" blocks of flats began to appear above the fairly low skyline of London and other English cities and continued to do so into the 1970s. But they did not do very much towards stopping the spread of houses. Most English people live in houses because they like living in houses. If they have to live in flats, they make the best of it; but there are very few who would not live in a house if they were given the chance, even if living in a house meant more work, less shops "right on the doorstep", and more time and money spent on bus, train and car travel.

Nor are they content with just the house. They like some garden to go with it, and some garden does go with most English houses, though it may well be only a narrow flower border round a small patch of grass. Many house-dwellers find that the small patch of grass is quite enough, too. Like

A housing estate in a "new" town— a development specially built to provide accommodation for people from overcrowded and uncomfortable city areas

English farm crops, grass is quick to grow during the warm summer months and it needs frequent cutting to keep it neat and stop it from smothering the flowers.

Something else that goes with many English houses is a dog, or a cat, or both. Very few English people feel properly at home without a pet of some kind, and those who can manage without one are inclined to think that the others have far too many—especially dogs, However, most dog-owners keep their dogs well-trained, well-controlled and very much at home except when they are taken for a walk on a lead, or given a run somewhere well away from traffic. Whether or not such a house-bound life can be good for the dogs is another matter.

Some of them do seem over-petted and under-exercised. But at least they are well looked after, and safer from traffic accidents than the freer dogs of some other countries.

The houses in which English dogs spend so much of their time are usually two-storied, and built of red brick, or of stone covered with stucco and painted. Wooden houses are rare, and hardly ever seen in towns. For people who still prefer the glow from an open fireplace to an electric heater in winter, there is too much fire risk in wooden buildings. Londoners found that out in 1666, the year of their Great Fire. Much of the city was then built of wood, and the fire spread from building to building through four hundred streets, leaving everything wooden in ashes, and everything else scorched, cracked and useless.

Besides, modern England has very little room to grow trees for timber. Most of its timber, and many of its timber products, must be imported. That can make building in wood a very expensive business. Stone is expensive, too, even though it need not be imported. So England's many stone houses are mainly fairly old ones. Bricks, or sometimes more modern materials like cement blocks, are used for most new houses.

Especially near the crowded centres of towns and in the older factory areas, English houses are often joined in terraces that fill a whole street with house-fronts that look exactly the same as each other. Where there is rather more land to spare, they are semi-detached—"Siamese twin" houses joined by a common central wall. With more land still, they become

Blenheim Palace in Oxfordshire and part of its beautiful gardens. This is one of many houses which are cared for by their owners and an organisation known as the National Trust. They are stately homes which are open to visitors

detached—each house standing free in its own grounds, with plenty of room for the dog to run, and perhaps more grass than the owner can control without the help of a motor-mower. But whether they are big or small, detached, semi-detached or terraced, nearly all English houses have one feature in common—a roof pitched steeply enough to carry away the rain that is so often falling, and to stop snow from piling thickly.

England was the home of the first successful experiments in television. It was also the home of the world's first regular television service, begun by the British Broadcasting Corporation in 1936. Since then television has become by far the most popular home entertainment for English people—too popular so some of them think. They say that it keeps people away from the reading, hobbies and indoor games that used to occupy them, and even stops family conversation. But in the winter at any rate there should be plenty of time for all those things and some television too. Winter evenings are long in England. Children are hardly home from school before daylight is fading, and it is well after dark when their fathers—and sometimes their mothers—come back from work.

During summer, the evenings are different. Daylight saving time adds an hour to summer daylight that is naturally long

Some old houses still show the use of timber. These half-timbered houses are in Chester

because of England's high latitude. So it is around ten o'clock or even later when darkness falls. And on dry evenings television loses many of its audience to outdoor games, or some work in the garden, or giving the car a wash.

There are now nearly as many cars in England as there are television sets, and that means something like one car for every eighteen yards (sixteen metres) of road. It also means that some families who own cars do not use them as much as they might. Parking places in towns can be so hard to find that many people travel by bus or train, and leave the car at home —often under a weatherproof cover in the street outside. Only the newest houses are fairly sure to have garages, and many of the older houses have too little space to add them.

Beautiful stone houses in Bath

Houses built from brick, with steeply pitched roofs, typical of English towns and cities (in the foreground is York Minster)

English people not only like to live in houses. They also like to own the houses they live in. Not all of them can manage that, but nearly half the houses in the country are owned by the people who live in them. Of the rest, more than half are "council houses"—houses built by and owned by local government councils, and let at weekly rents which do not put any great strain on the tenants' wages, or sometimes actually sold at a reasonable price to the people who have been renting them.

England has some national foods and national dishes that can be very good indeed if they are prepared with fresh English ingredients in a home kitchen. No visitor should miss the chance to try home-made steak pudding, apple pie, fruit cake or Cornish pasties. (Cornish pasties are a mixture of meat and vegetables wrapped in half-circles of pastry. They can be eaten from the hand, and so shops often sell them as snacks. But shop pasties are rarely good samples.)

Lancashire hot-pot—layers of meat and vegetables soaked in meat stock and cooked slowly in an oven—is another dish worth trying if it is home-made. So too is the famous Yorkshire pudding, a baked batter served with slices of roast beef, baked potatoes and gravy. Then there are the Devonshire teas that the travel agent advertised. English cafés offer many kinds of doubtful product under the name Devonshire tea, but the real one is hot home-made scones, cream fresh from the dairy, and strawberry jam that contains nothing but whole strawberries and sugar.

Tea, by the way, can be a very confusing meal for a visitor. He goes to tea with one family—especially in the south—and some time in the late afternoon he is offered a cup of tea, a scone or some bread and butter with jam, a piece of cake, and perhaps in the winter a slice of toast or a crumpet, hot and buttered. But with another family—especially in the north— he will wait until early evening and then sit down to a large meal, perhaps Lancashire hot-pot or fish and chips and then a sweet pudding. The first family might have that kind of meal even later—between seven and eight o'clock—and call it dinner or supper. But to the second family "dinner" is what the first family calls "luncheon" or "lunch"—a hot meal in the middle of the day—and supper is a very light meal, sometimes no more than a drink and a biscuit, just before bed.

That leaves breakfast as the only meal of the day that has the same name everywhere in England, and breakfast usually has the same menu everywhere in England. It begins with hot porridge or a cold pre-cooked cereal with sugar and milk, continues with eggs, a light meat dish or fish, and ends with toast and marmalade. There is also tea or coffee, of course— usually tea, but coffee has become more popular in recent years. Many visitors find such a large meal too large at the

The modern English housewife does much of her food shopping in supermarkets like this one

beginning of the day, and some English people agree with them. They prefer to leave out one or even two of the courses, but most would rather eat less later in the day than do without their breakfast. They say that a big breakfast sets them up for the day's work, and keeps them healthy.

Whether or not big breakfasts do keep the English people healthy is a matter for argument. But there can be no doubt that a free—or very nearly free—national medical service does much to keep them in good health. England is a welfare state, which means that everyone is entitled to medical treatment without doctors' bills, dental and optical treatment at no charge for children and reduced charges for adults, enough money to live on if he is unemployed, and a pension when he retires from work. To cover the cost of unemployment benefits, pensions, and an allowance for mothers with young children, everybody who is working pays a weekly contribution from his wages to an insurance fund. But the health services are paid for by the government, out of taxes. And it is from taxes too that local government councils, controlled and helped by the national government, provide free education for all children until they are at least sixteen years of age.

England at School

Free and compulsory education for all children was not one of England's "firsts". Even the Industrial Revolution did not hurry it along very quickly, although many more people who could at least read and write and do some arithmetic were needed for the new factory industries. In fact, it was not until 1870 that every English child could feel sure that he would go to school.

England had some free schools before 1870, and many other schools which gave free places to very clever children. But those schools were provided mainly by churches, or by rich people who liked to be helpful with their money. There were never enough for all children; and, even if there had been enough, all children would not have attended. Many parents saw no reason for sending their children to school. Many other parents earned such low wages that their children also had to work for money. Some stories by the English writers Charles Dickens and Charles Kingsley told luckier people what life was like for some of those children. They helped to make England see that the welfare of children should be a task for the government. At the same time, wages were becoming a little higher because the new manufacturing industries were making England much more prosperous. The prosperity also meant that richer people could pay higher taxes. So by 1870 there was nothing to stop the government from making education free and compulsory.

At first, it was compulsory only for younger children. After they had learned to read and write and do arithmetic they could leave school, and those who wanted more education had to pay for it. But in modern England no one is allowed to leave school until he is sixteen, and those who wish to stay longer may do so without any payment.

At the other end of the age range, some English children now start school when they are very young indeed. There are many nursery schools whose youngest children are only two years old, but at that age education is not compulsory. Most nursery school children come from families with working mothers who cannot be at home during the day, and who think that a child is better at school with others of his own age than in the care of relations or friends.

Compulsory education begins with primary schools, whose children are aged between five and eleven. There is hardly a village in England without its primary school, although children from some of the very small villages are taken by bus to a bigger village near by. The school day lasts from nine o'clock in the morning until somewhere between three and four o'clock in the afternoon, but the children need not take

64

Schoolchildren outside one of England's most modern comprehensive schools

their midday meal with them. Hot midday meals—meat, vegetables and a sweet pudding eaten at tables—are provided by the local government education authority, but they are free only for children whose parents cannot afford to pay, perhaps because they are unemployed. Other children pay for each meal.

Children leave primary school at the end of the summer term—late July—in the year of their eleventh birthday, and after a long summer holiday move to a secondary school in September.

Until fairly recently, there were three kinds of free school for secondary education. They were called secondary modern schools, grammar schools and comprehensive schools.

Secondary modern schools were mainly for pupils who intended to leave school and start work as soon as they were sixteen. Grammar schools were for pupils who intended to take examinations which could lead to the universities, or to training for work such as nursing, accountancy and teaching. Comprehensive schools provided secondary education for both the "grammar" and the "secondary-modern" types of pupil. However, schools of the comprehensive type have now replaced grammar and secondary modern schools in nearly every part of England.

In some countries, schools provided by the government are called public schools, but in England that would cause even more confusion than the different times and types of food for the meal called tea. To English people, a public school is one of the several types of school *not* provided by the government. It is a secondary school—very often a boarding school—for pupils aged between thirteen and nineteen, whose parents are willing to pay for their education. Most public schools began long before the time of free and compulsory education, some many centuries before. The earliest of them were founded when the only schools in England were local day schools for boys in some of the bigger towns. To attend a local school, a boy had to live in the town or the district around it. But the public schools offered to take boarding pupils from anywhere in the

A view of Christchurch College, Oxford

country. That is why they were given the now confusing name "public schools".

Although public schools charge fees, nobody makes any money from them. If there is any money left over at the end of a school year, it is used for improving the school. For that reason, public schools are different from some other English schools which charge fees. The other schools are run as businesses, and among them are many of the fee-charging primary schools—called preparatory schools—attended by children who will go to public schools when they are old enough.

Until 1832, England had only two universities. They were

67

the ancient and famous universities of Oxford and Cambridge, whose beautiful buildings should be seen by every visitor, and whose annual boat race may be seen by any visitor who on the first Saturday of April happens to be anywhere between Putney and Mortlake on the River Thames. However, new universities followed the Industrial Revolution much more closely than free primary schools. The first of the new ones was opened in 1832 at Durham, an old city built around a hilltop castle on the coalfields of the north-east. Next, in 1836, came the University of London, which allows its examinations to be taken by students overseas, and so has provided a university education for thousands of people in Commonwealth countries without universities of their own. Two more—both in the new industrial areas—were opened before primary education became free and compulsory, and there are now thirty-six, most of them in areas where there are very large numbers of people, and some with over ten thousand students.

All thirty-six universities are open to anyone who can qualify for a place in them, but university education is not completely free. Instead, for each year of every student's course, the government gives him a grant of money, and the size of the grant depends upon the amount of his parents' income.

There is also a new and very unusual university—mainly for older students who study in their spare time—called the Open University. Like the overseas students of London University, students of the Open University study at home. But they see

68

and hear a good deal of their teachers, all the same. Lectures and demonstrations are broadcast on the sound and television networks of the British Broadcasting Corporation, at times which are carefully planned to suit all students. The students have to pay for their courses, but they are not charged very much. A grant from the government through its Department of Education and Science pays a large part of the university's expenses.

Of course, it should not be forgotten that the government education system, like the welfare services and council housing, belongs to the whole of the United Kingdom. What England has, Scotland, Wales and Northern Ireland have too, and all four countries have shared in making it. So the wage-earners of all four countries also benefit from some very popular laws that limit their working hours, and oblige their employers to give them at least two weeks' paid holiday every year.

England at Leisure

It was an Englishman who wrote the song *I do like to be beside the seaside*, and the song says what most English people still feel when they are thinking about their annual holidays. Even when they holiday abroad they go mainly to seaside places, but there is no need for them to go abroad if all they want is the sea. England itself is a very fine country for seaside holidays if the weather keeps dry and warm; and it often is dry and warm for much of late July and early August, the main holiday period.

The largest numbers of seaside holiday-makers come from the crowded industrial areas, so it may seem rather surprising that many of them spend their seaside holidays in places that are equally crowded. They choose very big seaside towns like Blackpool in Lancashire and Southend near London, where there are plenty of fun-fairs, dance-halls and pier entertainments, and an endless supply of ice-cream and the pink and white sweet called rock.

Those who like a quieter time may go to fishing harbours and little rocky coves in the West Country, where the smugglers of adventure stories used to land contraband from France, or to long stretches of open, sandy beach on the North Sea coast. There are also islands—the Scillies off Cornwall, where the climate is so warm that spring flowers are sent from there to London markets in the middle of winter; the Channel Islands where many of the people are French and still speak

A Punch and Judy
show—a
traditional
English seaside
entertainment

French; the Isle of Man in the Irish Sea, where visitors who arrive at the right time of the year may see some of the world's best motor-cyclists competing in a very difficult up hill and down dale race.

Whether they choose the seaside or not, English people usually like to get out in the open air during their annual holidays. There is, of course, plenty of open air away from the seaside. Walkers who like a really long walk may spend their whole holiday following the Pennine Way, a 250-mile (400-kilometre) footpath over the whole length of the Pennine Range. If they prefer to walk in shorter stretches, they can try

71

A south-coast resort—calm sea, sandy beach, well-built promenade and pier with entertainments

the wild wastes of Dartmoor in south Devon, or the smoother and more settled Exmoor in north Devon and Somerset. Exmoor is the scene of the story *Lorna Doone*, and the home of wild deer and the little brown Exmoor ponies. Every autumn, some of the ponies are rounded up and sold with other ponies during a noisy and crowded street fair in the village of Bampton—once a prosperous wool town—at the southern edge of the moor. Buyers who want to make sure that they are sold a real Exmoor pony can recognize them by a band of oatmeal-coloured hair around the mouth. They look as though they have been eating from an oatmeal sack, and have taken too big a mouthful.

There are also ponies and deer in the New Forest, a wide area of thinly-wooded country inland from the seaport city of Southampton, on the English Channel coast. New Forest ponies are handsome, but often dangerous. In spite of warnings, some visitors to the forest unwisely give them buns and biscuits and chocolate. That makes them expect food from all visitors, and they are inclined to kick or bite those who do not offer it.

Apart from deer, ponies and a few wild white cattle, England's wild animals are not very noticeable. There is no wild animal bigger than the fox, and all are too shy to wait while visitors look at them, even if the visitors do offer buns. Foxes are especially quick to get out of the way. Much to the distress of many English people, some others hunt foxes—and also deer—in a way that seems very cruel.

Bird-life is much more obvious. England has over four hundred kinds of bird, most very noticeable because of their noise if not because of their size. Birdwatching is a popular holiday occupation. Some of the more common birds may be seen almost anywhere, but serious birdwatchers choose places where there is a chance of finding the rarer kinds. Among those places are the reserve of the Wildfowl Trust at Slimbridge on the River Severn, and the Norfolk Broads, an area of coastal lakes and marshes not far from Norwich.

Ponies in the New Forest

The Broads are also very popular among those who like to spend their holidays "messing about in boats". Others prefer what many people think is the most beautiful part of England, the mountainous Lake District in the north-west. There, they may climb England's highest mountains, a little over three thousand feet (one thousand metres), if they want to have some time off the water.

For boating holiday-makers who enjoy seeing some of England's most interesting towns, there are the canals and the many navigable rivers. From the Thames they can visit Oxford—a very quiet town when the nine thousand students are themselves on holiday—and see the long streets lined with ancient university buildings, the little River Cherwell that

74

divides the old part of the town from the new industrial part, and the deer herd in the grounds of Magdalen College. From the Severn they can visit Worcester —which really does make Worcestershire sauce—and see a county cricket match on the riverside cricket ground, a chinaware factory that is one of the few serious competitors of the kilns in the Potteries, and a cathedral which shows the different building styles of four centuries, because it took over four hundred years to complete. From the Warwickshire Avon they can visit Stratford and see the house where Shakespeare is supposed to have been born, the house where he really did live, and some of his plays being performed by England's best actors at the riverside Royal Shakespeare Theatre. From the Regent's Canal, which goes almost to the centre of London, they can visit London's famous Regent's Park zoo. From any of a dozen other rivers

Derwentwater, one of the most beautiful areas in the Lake District

and canals they can land in towns of all ages and sizes with equally interesting things to show. Indeed, many people live near enough to rivers or canals to make more boating journeys over the weekends between annual holidays.

For most English people, the weekend is all day Saturday and Sunday. But for some—including some school-children— it is Saturday afternoon and all day Sunday. To make up for the lost Saturday morning, many of those have a free afternoon during the week. For everybody there are public holidays spread throughout the year, though not as many as there are in some other countries. Four of the public holidays—Easter Monday, May Day, the Spring Holiday (once called Whit

The Royal Shakespeare Theatre, Stratford-upon-Avon, home of the Royal Shakespeare Company

Monday) and the August Bank Holiday—always fall on a Monday, giving England four long weekends every year. The four long weekends come at the beginning, the middle, and the end of the warmer months, and so are times for many special outdoor events and activities, including agricultural shows, folk-dancing displays, carnivals, some of the main cricket and football matches, and a cheese race. In the cheese race, held at a small village in Gloucestershire, runners chase a huge round cheese as it rolls down a hill, and the runner who catches it keeps it.

But, of course, there are outdoor events and activities at ordinary weekends, too—especially on Saturdays. Sunday is a quiet day in England, when most people like to sleep late in the morning, and take life easily for the rest of the day. Some go to church, or tune in to church services broadcast on television and sound radio. Nearly all have a bigger and slower midday meal than usual, and spend at least some of the time before it reading Sunday newspapers. The English are very fond of their newspapers on any day of the week, but on Sundays they buy more than twice as many as they do on other days. However, they can buy very little else on Sunday, except meals in restaurants, drinks, and foodstuffs—including sweets. The law obliges most places of business, as well as many places of entertainment, to keep closed on Sundays, and many of those that could stay open do not.

Saturdays are much more lively, and Saturday afternoons are the main time for the many outdoor games which large numbers of English people either play or watch. Easily the most popular games are the three kinds of football—Association, often called soccer, Rugby Union, usually called rugger, and Rugby League. In soccer, the ball is round, and no player except the goalkeeper may pick it up, or even touch it with his hands. In the Rugby games, the ball is oval, and any player may pick it up and run with it as far as the other team will let him. Football began as a winter game, but soccer is now so popular that there are less than four months of the year when no matches are played, and even in those months boys— and girls—may be seen kicking a ball about in playgrounds, in side streets and on the beaches.

Next to football, the most popular outdoor activity of the winter is a single event—Guy Fawkes' Night. On 5th November 1605, a man named Guy Fawkes was caught trying to kill King James I and his ministers by blowing up the Houses of Parliament in London. So, on every 5th November, people all over England stuff old clothes to make a dummy called a guy. And then after dark they burn it in as big a bonfire as they can build, to the accompaniment of fireworks. To pay for fireworks, children often carry or wheel a guy through the streets, asking people to give them "a penny for the guy".

After Guy Fawkes' Night, people rarely stay out of doors on winter nights unless they have to, or unless they go carol-singing on Christmas Eve. Carol-singers usually ask for money, too—sometimes for themselves, more often for

Playing rugger in an English park

charities. When they sing outside a house, the people who live in it may also give them something to eat—perhaps some of the small sweet mince pies that the English like to eat on Christmas Eve.

In spite of stories and the pictures on so many Christmas cards, the English Christmas is very rarely a white one. It is much more likely to be a wet one. But everything else from the stories and the pictures is there—the Christmas trees and the decorations in houses and shopping centres, the church bells on Christmas morning, the brightly wrapped presents, the roast turkey and the holly-topped Christmas pudding, the candles and the crackers and the party hats. And on Boxing Day—another public holiday, on the day after Christmas

Day—there is the pantomime for those who have been able to book seats. Those who have not will find their chance later. The Boxing Day performances are the first of many.

A pantomime was originally an actor who performed with actions alone, and used no words at all. But, as has happened so often with words from other languages, the English language has given the word pantomime a new meaning. The English pantomime is not an actor, but a play, and a play which uses a very large number of words, some spoken, some sung. The story of the play is always one of the old fairy tales or folk tales —perhaps *Cinderella*, or the adventures of the poor country boy Dick Whittington, who walked to London and eventually became the city's lord mayor with the help of a remarkable cat. And the hero's part is always played by a young woman dressed in a man's clothes, while the principal comedian is always a man dressed as a woman.

There are very few English towns where a pantomime of some kind is not performed during the last week of the old year and the first week of the new. But the really spectacular ones, with the country's most popular comedians and huge casts of singers and dancers, are mainly to be found in the theatres of London. Midwinter is also a good time for English people to see London's many museums and art galleries, and such London attractions as the changing of the guard at Buckingham Palace and Madame Tussaud's waxworks. There is more room to see them in winter, because the summer brings so many visitors from overseas. So, in the week or two after Christmas, when most schools are still on holiday, many English families follow Dick Whittington to England's capital city.

The Christmas Tree in Trafalgar Square, London, which is sent each year from Norway (in the foreground is the famous statue of Lord Nelson)

England's Mighty Heart

If you read in a guide book that the City of London has 4,234 people, you have not found a misprint. The book is talking about the real London, the old city that covers only about one square mile (just over $2\frac{1}{2}$ square kilometres) of the 610 square miles (1,580 square kilometres) covered by modern London.

Nowadays, the old city is nearly all taken up by banks and office buildings. That is why so few people live in it. It is also why visitors rarely go there except to see a very colourful procession called the Lord Mayor's Show, and two historic buildings—the huge, domed cathedral of St. Paul, built after an earlier cathedral was destroyed in the Great Fire of 1666, and the Tower of London, begun by the Norman kings who made London the capital of England.

Although it is hard to tell where one starts and the other begins, the area that attracts most visitors is a different city altogether, the City of Westminster. Westminster contains Buckingham Palace, the Houses of Parliament, the biggest shops, the National Art Gallery, the British Museum, much of London University, the main theatres, the most popular parks and squares, and the Abbey church where British monarchs are crowned, and where many of the greatest people from England's past are buried. It also contains about half of a wide riverside road called the Victoria Embankment, along which are moored some famous "retired" ships that are open

82

Trooping the Colour—one of England's traditional displays of the discipline and skill of her soldiers

to visitors. One of them is *Discovery*, in which the explorer Robert Falcon Scott made a voyage to Antarctica.

The river, of course, is the Thames. From Westminster, near the Houses of Parliament and the famous clock Big Ben, it is crossed by Westminster Bridge. Like the present Houses of Parliament, Westminster Bridge is not much more than a hundred years old. But there was an earlier bridge at Westminster, opened in 1750. It was from that bridge that the poet William Wordsworth took a sweeping look at the London of the early nineteenth century and wrote a poem in which he called it "that mighty heart".

Even as late as Wordsworth's time, the "mighty heart" was very much smaller than it is now. One of Westminster's best-known churches is called St. Martin-in-the-Fields because

Part of the "mighty heart"; London's Oxford Street with its shops, crowds, red buses and typical London taxis

it had stood among fields not long before. And beyond Westminster the now busy and densely-peopled area of Kensington consisted mainly of a few very grand country houses. But in one way Wordsworth's London was more truly the heart of England than modern London is. The big cities that grew with the Industrial Revolution and became important centres of industry, commerce and population had barely started growing. Because London was the seat of government and the main outlet to the continent of Europe, it had become the one important centre for all England. Many English people still say that they are "going to town" when they set out for London, even though they may pass through cities as big as Manchester and Birmingham on the way.

84

For them at least, London is still the "mighty heart" of the country. And although it is no longer the *one* important centre, it is still the chief important centre. That is partly because it has remained the seat of government, but even more because of something that people often forget. Although central London is thirty-seven miles (sixty kilometres) from the mouth of the Thames, the river is wide and deep all the way, and the city is England's chief seaport. Also, because England for a long time had the largest fleet of merchant ships in the world, London was the largest seaport in the world. It is still nearly the world's largest, with anchorages and docks stretching twenty-six miles (forty kilometres) down both sides of the river from London Bridge to Tilbury, where the biggest ocean-going ships land their cargoes and passengers.

By the way, London Bridge is not, as some visitors think, the very tall drawbridge often seen in pictures. That is Tower Bridge, near the Tower of London. Nor is the present London Bridge, a little further up the river, the bridge of the old song

British cars being produced by robots at a factory just outside London

London bridge is falling down. The bridge of the song, a stone bridge with wooden shops and houses built along its sides, managed not to fall down for six hundred years, and was then pulled down to make way for a stronger one without shops and houses. But even the stronger one proved too weak and narrow for modern traffic. It has now been replaced by a bridge of concrete, and its stones have been taken to the United States, and put together to make a bridge over a river there.

If you look at a map of England's railways, you will see that every main line in the country leads to London. If the map shows airports, you will also see that the main airports are in the London area. Both those things have helped London to keep its place as England's most important and thickly-populated centre. It has also kept ahead of the growing industrial cities by developing some of the same industries that caused them to grow. For example, Dagenham, an industrial suburb on the north side of the Thames, rivals Coventry in the making of motor vehicles. And at least some of nearly everything else that England makes is made somewhere in the vast area of modern London, since 1963 called Greater London to distinguish it from the old city around St. Paul's Cathedral.

London also remains the "mighty heart" of England because it is the centre not only for Christmas pantomimes, but also for entertainment of all kinds and for cultural life. New plays and films from all over the world, and the best

London's theatreland

productions of old plays, are usually seen in London before the rest of England sees them. There is constant music, ranging from the bands of the Guards regiments playing near the wildfowl pond in St. James's Park to grand opera at Covent Garden. The Opera House stands near what was once a famous flower, fruit and vegetable market. But that has now been moved to Nine Elms, up river on the other side of the River Thames. The British Broadcasting Corporation and the Independent Broadcasting Authority, which provide all of the United Kingdom's television and sound radio, both have their headquarters in London. So too have all the national newspapers and most book, magazine and music publishers. England's main art galleries and art dealers are London galleries and dealers. And London has the best-known schools of acting, music and dancing; the best free libraries in a country that has good free libraries nearly everywhere; the largest number of well-stocked museums, and the widest range of interesting buildings from all periods of England's history.

The interesting buildings include many very modern ones, among them the Post Office tower, 580 feet (190 metres) high. Modern buildings are more noticeable in London than in many of the world's other great cities because the central area lost about one-third of its older buildings in the air-raids of the Second World War. That is also the main reason why parts of some smaller English cities have a very modern look. Some of London's new buildings are not well-liked, partly because their appearance is displeasing to many people, and partly because they tend to crowd in on other more familiar buildings.

Unpopular new buildings aside, English people sometimes feel that London has too many of the best things. They say that it would be better for the country if some of them were shared with the other big centres. But, for others, London's chief attraction is that so much is concentrated there. And, as more than one-third of the English people can easily get "to town" for an afternoon or an evening, it is not surprising that the concentration continues. Nor is it surprising that when changes come to England, they very often spread from London.

Changing England

The English have often described themselves as a conservative people. That does not mean that a majority of them always vote for parliamentary candidates belonging to the political groups called the Conservative Party. What it does mean is that they are—or like to think that they are—slow to make changes, and inclined to do things or to keep things only because those things have been kept or done for a long time.

A visitor may well agree with them when he sees the boys of a Bristol school wearing uniforms of the same design as those worn when the school was founded four hundred years ago,

Tradition preserved. Morris dancers outside Wells Cathedral, Somerset

or a judge in the law courts being presented with a posy of flowers because the smell of flowers was supposed to stop people from catching a deadly plague that struck England in 1348. Indeed, for many visitors such carefully preserved links with the past are one of England's chief attractions. It is not every country where by ancient law the head of state owns exactly two-thirds of all the swans on the main river, and once a year has them all rounded up for counting; or where groups of men in costumes of the past perform old folk-dances in the streets on public holidays; or where anyone going through a particular cathedral town may ask for the free bread and beer that has been given to wayfarers for eight centuries.

But that is only one side of the English. In other ways, they are not nearly so conservative as they seem. After all, it was the English who began the changes which shaped and equipped modern industry. And it was changes forced by the English which gave other nations a pattern for parliamentary government. So visitors should not be misled by judges with posies, and swan uppings (countings), and street-dancing bank clerks wearing ribboned hats and knee-bells. Those things are only a pleasant permanent background to changes which are always going on, and with which most English people manage to move quite comfortably, however "conservative" they may think themselves.

Since the Second World War, the changes have been big and wide indeed, perhaps bigger and wider than any since the English grew used to the Industrial Revolution. Some of

90

The annual swan-upping (counting) on the River Thames

those changes are the coming of the welfare state, for example, and the large number of Indian, Pakistani and West Indian immigrants who have given a new look to some of the big cities, especially London.

Perhaps the biggest changes of all are some which are still far from complete. Those are the changes which must come because England and the other countries of the United

Kingdom have joined the European Common Market—or, to give it its official name, the European Economic Community. Membership of the Common Market means that in many ways the English will now be much more closely linked with the peoples of western Europe than with the English-speaking peoples of the British Commonwealth and the United States of America. That will surely make the England of the year 2000 very different from the England of 1950. For more than a thousand years the English people have shown that they are very good at accepting such changes whilst still remaining English. A visitor in the year 2000 is still likely to find them counting swans.

Index